THE MOSAIC PROJECT BOOK
MOROCCAN STYLE
KATRINA HALL

Mosaic design has often been described as 'painting by numbers' and, however basic a description this might be, it does provide a clue to this art form's key attraction – its accessibility. Mosaics are simply the creation of patterns and pictures from pieces of stone, ceramics, porcelain or glass . . . what could be simpler?

The designs range from very simple to very detailed – both can be beautiful. Start with straightforward designs and, as you gain in confidence, move onto more ambitious projects. Experiment with different materials and designs.

You will soon discover why mosaics have existed as an art form for over 2,000 years – some even date the earliest examples of mosaics back to Ancient Mesopotamia in around 3,000 BC. The combination of their decorative and functional attributes ensured the future of mosaics as a versatile and durable art form that will always have an ageless appeal. All you need to enjoy mosaic design is time, patience and imagination.

MATERIALS

Tesserae (which comes from the Latin word for 'square' and Greek word for 'four') is the name of the pieces used to make mosaics. They come in all manner of shapes and sizes and are supplied on sheets or loose. When storing tesserae, you need to make them easily identifiable, so glass or transparent containers are ideal for loose cubes and clearly labelled boxes work well for flat sheets. All adhesives, cements and additives are best stored in a dry, cool place.

Below is a list of the main materials used in mosaic design. However, there are no rules and mosaicists can use any number of other materials including glass beads, buttons, coins, shells, slate, semi-precious stones and broken household china.

Marble tesserae Available in a natural palette of colours, marble tesserae have either polished or unpolished finishes: the former gives a smooth elegant finish whereas the latter has a more rustic look. Cut marble using a hammer and hardie (see page 4) and protect with a sealant. Commonly used pieces are 1.5 x 1.5cm ($^5/_8$ x $^5/_8$in).

Vitreous glass Available in a range of colours and palettes, these are relatively cheap and resistant to heat and frost making them ideal for both interior and exterior use. Cut glass using mosaic nippers (see page 4). They are usually supplied in single colour sheets of 2 x 2cm ($^3/_4$ x $^3/_4$in) or loose in mixed bags.

Porcelain These are usually supplied unglazed and are available in a wide range of shades. Suited to both internal and external application, they offer excellent 'slip'-resistant properties even when wet. Use mosaic nippers for cutting (see page 4) and follow the advice of your tile supplier with regard to sealants.

Ceramic These are similar to porcelain tesserae except that they are usually glazed.

Smalti These are made from glass, which are prepared and cut into rectangular strips and then into rectangular tesserae. Smalti reflect light beautifully due to irregularities caused by hand-cut glass surfaces. Sold by the 500g (1lb) or 1kg (2lbs) usually in pieces of 1 x 1.5cm ($^1/_2$ x $^5/_8$in), smalti are quite expensive but worth every penny! They can be used internally and externally because they are heat and frost proof. Use a hammer and hardie to cut smalti (see page 4).

Gold or silver leaf These tesserae are made when a thin layer of 24-carat gold, or silver, is hammered onto a coloured glass backing and covered with a film of veneer glass. These are then hand cut into tesserae, which can lead to irregularities in sizes and shapes. Either plain or rippled, these should be used sparingly for decorative purposes only because the silver or gold breaks down in excessive conditions, such as extreme heat and frost.

Pebbles or stones Available in a variety of colours, sizes and textures, granite and hard stones are recommended for durability and can be used internally and externally.

Household ceramic tiles These come in a wonderful range of colours and sizes, and are very cheap, which makes experimental cutting affordable. Always check the durability of tiles because certain types are prone to cracking under extreme conditions.

Glass and mirror Use these to add a reflective quality to your mosaics. They are available in large panels from glass shops and some tile suppliers, and should be cut very carefully with a glass cutter.

BASIC TOOLS

The basic mosaicist tool kit can be very simple and you may already have most of this equipment around your home. If not, visit a hardware store, builders' merchant or tile supplier (see page 32).

1. Hardie Sometimes called a bolster blade, this is used with a hammer, for cutting marble and smalti. The hardie is a small metal block with an anvil-shaped edge, which can either be embedded in concrete in a flower pot or in an upright log.

2. Hammer This is curved on one edge and tipped with tungsten carbide. There are various weights of hammers – you should find one that is comfortable for you but that is in proportion with the hardie.

3. Mouth and nose filter masks Wear these when cutting tesserae, mixing grout and cement or using strong smelling solvents.

4. Mosaic nippers These are used to cut vitreous glass, porcelain and ceramic tesserae. The cutting edge is usually tipped with tungsten carbide for durability. Buy nippers with spring action handles to make cutting less arduous.

5. Tile cutters These cutters carve through tiles in a two-step process. On one part of the cutters is a small wheel or blade and on the other, a flat edge known as the snapper. First the tile is scored with the blade and then 'snapped' with the flat edge.

6. Electric drill This is used for fixing mosaic projects. Buy a selection of rawl plugs and screws and invest in a countersink bit, which hides screw heads. A jigsaw is also a useful tool for delicate, intricate cutting.

7. Gummed brown paper or brown paper One side of the former type is gummed, which, when damp, will bond tesserae temporarily making it ideal for the indirect method (see page 7). If you use brown paper, apply gum glue to the shiny side.

8. Wood Used as a base material or support, the type of wood you use will depend on the weight and size of your mosaic, and whether it will be featured indoors or outside. Always prime before use.

9. Paintbrush/glue spreaders These are to paint and prime surfaces.

10. Polyvinyl acetate (PVA) glue This is excellent for priming or preparing surfaces.

11. Tape measure/ruler Measuring tools.

12. Spirit level This has a liquid measure and, when the bubble is central, the surface measured is straight. Check surfaces are straight before mosaicing directly onto the walls.

13. Safety glasses Wear these when cutting tesserae as slivers can damage your eyes.

14. Scissors Cutting tool for paper/card.

15. Gum glue This is a water-based adhesive. It is normally used with brown paper in the indirect method (see page 7).

16. Tweezers These are wonderful for picking up small tesserae and placing them in position or for pricking out unwanted pieces.

17. Bradawl This makes an excellent 'prodder' or pricking-out implement, which removes unwanted cement and mosaics.

18. Stanley knife Cutting tool for paper/card.

19. String Useful for creating large circles.

20. Masking tape This is not as sticky as adhesive tape and so is ideal for attaching the template to tracing paper temporarily.

21. Graph paper and sketch pad These are especially useful during the design stages.

22. Markers, pens and pencils Use markers to draw your design on the base of the mosaic. Pens and pencils are essential throughout.

SAFETY ADVICE

When cutting:
▶ wear surgical gloves, safety glasses, mouth and nose filters
▶ wear closed-toe shoes
▶ lay dust sheets if working indoors

When applying adhesives, grouts or sealants:
▶ follow manufacturers' instructions
▶ wear surgical or rubber gloves
▶ work in well-ventilated areas and, if necessary, use mouth and nose filters
▶ wear an apron or overalls
▶ lay dust sheets

When drilling:
▶ always unplug when changing bits
▶ wear safety glasses

CUTTING AND SCORING

MOSAIC NIPPERS: These are used to cut vitreous glass and porcelain tesserae. Hold the nippers in one hand and the tesserae in the other. Before cutting, get used to handling the nippers, which should be held towards the bottom of the handles. Place the tesserae face up in between the cutting edges of the nippers and then apply firm pressure.

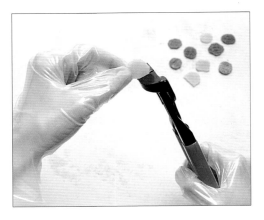

Cutting in half Place the tessera halfway into the mosaic nippers. Squeeze the handles firmly and the tessera will break in half. If you need quarters, take half a tessera and repeat the procedure. The quarters can also be cut in half to create smaller tesserae that are ideal for outlining.

Cutting diagonals Place the tessera diagonally into the cutting edges of the nippers. Apply pressure and the piece should cut forming two triangles.

Cutting curves or circles This shape is slightly more fiddly to perfect than halves or diagonals, but can be achieved if you nip off each of the corners of the tessera. Then slowly 'nibble' all the way around the tile in order to produce a smooth round circular or oval shape.

HAMMER AND HARDIE: Used to cut smalti and marble, this is similar to a tool used by the Romans. Make sure that your cutting hand is not restricted while you work and be patient because perfect results take time.

TILE CUTTERS: These are useful if you want to cut ceramic tiles that measure more than 2.5cm square (1in square) and are ideal if you are using spare tiles left over from the bathroom or kitchen. They have a dual function: first, the cutter blade scores a line along the tile and then the snappers break it. For ceramic squares, cut strips and then score and snap them into squares. You can get larger cutters or cutting machines for cutting thicker tougher tiles.

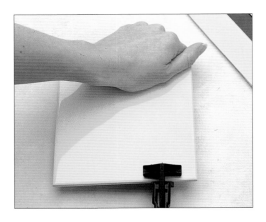

Hammer and hardie Position the tessera with your thumb and finger over the blade of the hardie where you want the cut to be. Then bring the hammer down lightly and firmly onto the centre of the tessera. Avoid inhaling dust by not cutting directly under your nose.

Scoring tiles In order to produce a scored line on your ceramic tile, place a metal rule in the exact position that you want the desired cutting line. Then run the tile cutter's blade along the metal rule applying even pressure as you go.

Snapping tiles Put the tile cutter's mouth over the centre of the scored line. Use your other hand to take the pressure away from the cut. Apply firm pressure to the cutters until you hear a 'snapping' noise when the tile is cut.

ADHESIVES, GROUTS AND TOOLS

There are different types of adhesives and grouts available but it is important that you choose the correct one for your project's requirements.

1. Polyvinyl acetate (PVA) glue (illustrated on page 3) A white glue that comes in two forms: water soluble and non-water soluble. The former can be used in the indirect method (see page 7). Also used to prime surfaces.

2. Gum glue (illustrated on page 3) This is usually water soluble and is used for the indirect method (see page 7).

3. Cement-based adhesives These are available in powder, ready-mixed or rapid setting forms. Using an additive will allow more movement and flexibility.

4. Mortar mix (not illustrated) Made from sand, cement and water, this is ideal for making an exterior floor mosaic. The ratio is generally 3:1, sharp sand to cement.

5. Grout Used to fill the gaps between the tesserae, this comes in ready-mixed or powder form and a variety of colours. Illustrated here is the cement-based powder form. Ready-made products are also available but they tend to leave a residue behind.

6. Epoxy Grout (not illustrated) This is a two-part resin-based grout, which creates a waterproof barrier.

7. Paint Scraper This can be used to mix and apply small amounts of adhesive and grout.

8. Notched trowel This is used for laying the cement. It has a serrated or notched edge that combs the bed of cement, ensuring an even layer and creating a good key. A 3mm (¼in) notched trowel is recommended for mosaics as it creates a smaller grooved bed.

9. Trowel Use a pointed-head trowel for applying cement in small awkward areas, and for measuring and mixing adhesive and grouts.

10. Margin trowel Square-headed trowel.

11. Palette knives Available in different shaped heads, this is a flexible tool that is great for applying adhesive or grout in small areas and to smooth and remove excess.

12. Protective gloves Use rubber gloves when cleaning and grouting and surgical gloves when applying adhesive and cutting tesserae.

13. Grout float Used for applying grout, especially on larger projects, it also removes grout residue. Use a squeegee as an alternative.

14. Cloth Use for polishing off grout residue.

15. Tiler's sponge Ideal for removing grout and cleaning. Use the sponge in circular movements to ensure an even coverage.

16. Sealants A wide variety of sealants are available – seek advice from a tile supplier for the product most suited to your project.

17. Additive for adhesive This is used with powdered adhesive and allows more natural movement. It is especially important when working on wood and floorboards.

18. Additive for grout This is used with the powdered grout and allows for flexibility. Read the label for safety advice.

19. Measuring jug This is used when measuring ratios of water, grout and adhesive.

MIXING CEMENT AND GROUT

Measuring ingredients Follow the manufacturers' instructions with regard to quantities and ratios of ingredients – you can use various measuring devices, such as one full trowel or one full measuring jug to represent one unit of material.

Adding water Pour the ingredients into a clean bucket. Slowly add water and additive, and mix with a trowel.

Smoothing the mixture Using a small trowel, mix the ingredients thoroughly. The texture should be quite smooth and free of lumps, neither too runny nor too thick.

DIRECT MOSAIC-LAYING METHOD

 As the name suggests, this method enables you to apply the tesserae 'directly' (face up) in situ. This technique is useful because it enables you to see the final work progress piece by piece. It tends to be used mostly in three-dimensional projects, on uneven surfaces, in mosaic murals and splashbacks. It is not recommended for flat surfaces because the results may be irregular.

1 Using abrasive paper and a block, remove the rough edges from your base of your choice – here, a piece of wood was used. Run over the face of the base to create a good key.

2 Paint the front and side edges with one coat of PVA glue to prime the surface. Make sure you clean your brush immediately after use, or it will become stiff.

3 While you are waiting for the glue to dry, you can start to cut the mosaic pieces (see page 4) and prepare your adhesive. Once the PVA has dried completely, draw on your design with a pencil or marker pen.

4 Spread the adhesive onto the base using a palette knife (or a notched trowel for large projects). Put your tesserae in place following the outline of the design. Allow the cement-based adhesive to dry for 24 hours.

5 Prick out excess cement with a bradawl or similar tool so that it will not show through the grout. Wash it away with a sponge and water. If using marble tesserae, apply a protective coating at this stage.

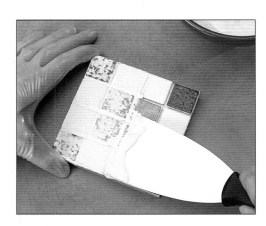

6 Put on rubber gloves and mix a quantity of grout (see page 5). Use a palette knife, squeegee or paint scraper to squeeze the grout in the gaps between the tiles.

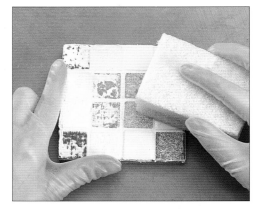

7 Remove the excess grout using a clean damp sponge. Repeat this process several times and regularly rinse your sponge to keep it clean and avoid smearing.

8 Use a cloth to polish the surface removing any residue. After the grout has dried for 24 hours, apply a sealant with a paintbrush or cloth.

INDIRECT MOSAIC-LAYING METHOD

The indirect method will enable you to lay the mosaic in reverse. Firstly, draw the design back to front on gummed brown paper and stick the tesserae in position. When the mosaic is complete on paper, apply it to the permanent base in a bed of cement. Wash off the backing paper to reveal the design, and grout. Use this method for flat surfaces and large projects.

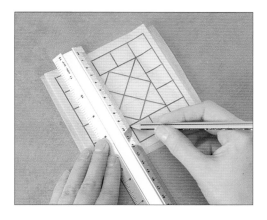

1 Draw your design with colour references. Trace onto tracing paper, turn it over and transfer onto gummed paper (sticky side up) or brown paper showing the design in reverse.

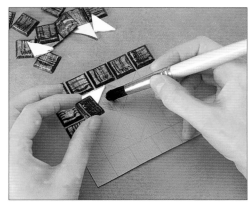

2 Stick the tesserae in position face down on the paper. For gummed paper, use water to bond the tesserae. For brown paper, use a water-soluble glue, such as gum glue.

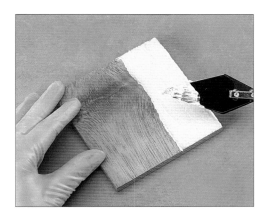

3 Prepare your adhesive-based cement using the method outlined on page 5. Apply to the surface using a paint scraper or a trowel for larger projects. Be sure to prime the surface before you begin, especially if using wood.

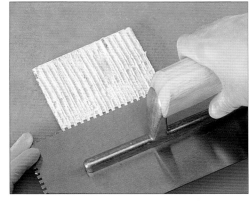

4 Drag a notched trowel at a 45-degree angle towards you in one sweeping action. This creates a grooved surface in the adhesive, which provides a good key in which the tesserae can bond.

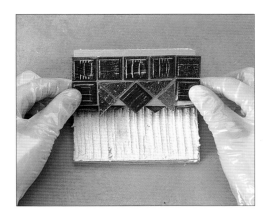

5 Carefully lift the mosaic and line its top edge with the top of the wood. Slowly lower the mosaic onto the adhesive bed. Smooth and press the tesserae with your hands. Leave to dry for 24 hours.

6 To reveal the design, moisten the paper with a wet sponge and then peel it off. Remove excess cement by pricking it out with a bradawl or similar tool. If using marble, apply a protective coating at this stage.

7 Wearing rubber gloves, prepare and apply grout, and remove any excess with a damp sponge. Rinse the sponge frequently to avoid smearing the grout instead of removing it. Leave to dry for 24 hours.

8 Polish the mosaic with a cloth to remove the fine layer of grout residue. If the mosaic is made of marble, make sure that you apply a coat of sealant using a cloth or paintbrush.

Cool Blue Splashback

MATERIALS AND TOOLS

2.5 x 2.5cm (1 x 1in) mottled
ceramic tiles (on webbing): one
sheet of each colour
Exterior plywood: 1cm (½in)
depth x 65cm (2⅛ft) length x
43cm (1⅓ft) width
Electric drill and countersink bit
PVA waterproof glue
Paintbrush
Tracing paper
Pencil
Ruler
Tile cutters
Surgical gloves and rubber gloves
Safety glasses
Mask
Two buckets for mixing
White exterior powder adhesive
and additive
Trowel
Bradawl or prodding tool
White exterior powder grout
and additive
Squeegee
Sponge
Cloth
Rawl plugs and screws

CERAMIC TILE COLOURS

Brilliant white – *Flores AF-3 [RH]*
Sky blue – *Harmonie Galapagos
AG-32 [RH]*
Turquoise – *Bahamas AG-75 [RH]*
(See page 32 for key to suppliers)

This stylish splashback has been created from glazed ceramic tiles with a glossy surface in soothing turquoise, sky blue and brilliant white. Blue and white were the original colours of ancient Moroccan mosaic, a palette brought from China by the Persians. Here they combine to produce a tranquil, peaceful bathroom. Created by laying tiles on the diagonal, this eye-catching pattern looks impressive but is simple to follow and requires little cutting. The ceramic tiles used here come with webbing on the back rather than paper. You can cut the sheets into sections and lay the mosaics in easy chunks or remove the backing altogether and use each tile individually. Whichever method you use, you will find this a quick and easy project that creates a stunning result.

USING THE TEMPLATE

Detach the template at the back of the book. Turn the tracing paper over and go over the outline on the reverse in pencil. Turn it back over and place it over the plywood. Trace over the front, transferring your design onto the board.

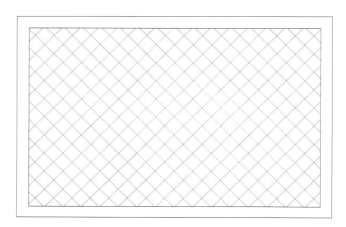

The blue tile border is not incorporated in the template and space should be allowed for it around the edge of the plywood.

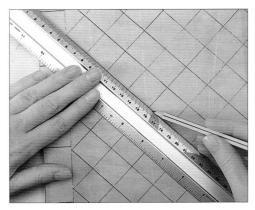

1 Take your chosen tiles and try varying their position within the square design. It is amazing how different the project can look by simply changing the colours around. Put together a number of designs and choose a favourite from these.

2 Using exterior plywood as your base, drill a hole in each corner. Then go over each hole with a countersink bit. Brush two coats of waterproof PVA glue on the front and back of the board to prime the surface.

3 Trace the design from the template directly onto the board and, if necessary, mark over the pencil line by hand to give a definite pattern to follow. Use a ruler to help ensure straight lines. Sticking down the template can help when tracing.

4 Count up the number of triangle pieces needed for the design. Score each tile using the tile cutters and snap in two. A quick precise action gives a much neater line than a slow cut – perhaps buy a few extra tiles to allow for mistakes.

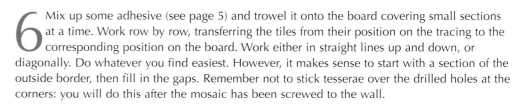

5 Remove the whole tiles from the webbing and group into colour piles. Spread out the tracing and place on the tiles ready for sticking to the board. The more accurate your placings are at this stage, the quicker the project will be finished.

6 Mix up some adhesive (see page 5) and trowel it onto the board covering small sections at a time. Work row by row, transferring the tiles from their position on the tracing to the corresponding position on the board. Work either in straight lines up and down, or diagonally. Do whatever you find easiest. However, it makes sense to start with a section of the outside border, then fill in the gaps. Remember not to stick tesserae over the drilled holes at the corners: you will do this after the mosaic has been screwed to the wall.

7 When the whole board is complete, check for any protruding tiles on the border and, if necessary, re-position them against the edge. Prick out loose adhesive with a bradawl while it is still wet – you may have to do this section by section. (As this is a large project you may not have time to complete the task in one sitting but do not be tempted to leave any adhesive unpicked.)

8 Mix up the grout (see page 5) and smear it on with a palette knife making sure you fill every little gap. Wipe clean the surface with a wet sponge. Leave to dry for 24 hours. Polish off the dusty residue from the surface with a dry cloth. See *Hints and Tips* (below) for instructions on how to fix the mosaic to the wall.

HINTS AND TIPS

▶ To help decide on the final colour configuration, hold a mirror against each square design as this will double the effect and give an idea of its repetitive appeal.

▶ This project uses large tesserae, although you could use standard size tiles if the template is scaled down. You can either do this yourself of take the template to a photocopy shop. Remember, the plywood needs to match the new template size.

▶ There can be a lot of colour variation in mottled tiles. When two or four tiles are linked together, check that there is not an odd one out that is much lighter or darker.

▶ If small holes appear when rubbing off the excess grout, simply run your finger along the grouted line to fill them in.

▶ After drilling holes in the wall, where you want your splashback to go, and fitting rawl plugs, screw the mosaic to the wall using a drill to fix the screws. Then mix up a small amount of adhesive, and stick the tesserae over the area covering the screws. Leave to dry for 24 hours. Prick out excess adhesive, then grout and wipe as described above.

INSPIRATIONAL IDEAS

This pattern could be adapted to work on a much

larger surface, for example, a shower basin or

bathroom floor. Simply reuse the template,

repeating the design over a greater area.

Vibrant Star
Water Dish

MATERIALS AND TOOLS

40cm (16in) flat-bottomed
terracotta dish
PVA waterproof exterior glue
Paintbrush
Tracing paper
Brown paper
Pencil
Scissors
2 x 2cm (¾ x ¾in) glass tesserae:
one sheet of red, half sheet of
black and deep orange, and three-
quarter sheet of tangerine orange
Tile cutters
Surgical gloves and rubber gloves
Safety glasses
Mask
Fine paintbrush
Two buckets for mixing
Black exterior powder adhesive
and additive
Notched plastic scraper
Trowel
Sponge
Bradawl or prodding tool
Masking tape
Black exterior powder grout
and additive
Squeegee
Cloth

GLASS TESSERAE COLOURS

Jet black – *20.77(3) [EU]*
Tangerine orange – *20.79(3) [EU]*
Deep orange – *20.99(3) [EU]*
Blood red – *D092 [MS]*
(See page 32 for key to suppliers)

Decorate a plain dish with intensely coloured glass tesserae, in a palette that evokes the exotic spice markets of Marrakesh. The intricate design works harmoniously with the bright hues, whereas the contrasting black grout highlights the colours. Although the pattern is quite complicated, if you tackle small sections at a time it is easily achieved, and as the overall project is quite small, it does not take long to complete. To relax away from the hubbub of everyday life, Moroccans often sit in the sanctuary of cool courtyards and float aromatic rose petals and flowers in their fountains. Emulate this custom by filling this stunning dish with water and floating your own choice of blooms. Or you might prefer to float scented candles across the surface to set the scene for a candlelit Moroccan dinner.

USING THE TEMPLATE

Detach the template from the back of the book. Turn the tracing over and go over the outline on the reverse in pencil. Turn the tracing back over and position it on brown paper. Trace over the front, transferring the design onto the brown paper. Cut out the dish shape, so that it fits inside the dish.

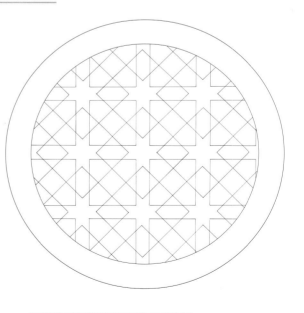

With a different sized dish you will have to reduce or enlarge the template accordingly to fit.

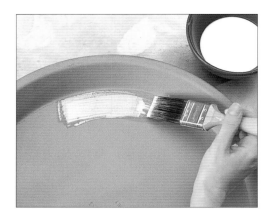

1 Give the terracotta dish two coats of PVA glue, inside and out, to make it water-resistant. Terracotta is very porous, so test how watertight the dish is by filling it with water and leaving it on the side of a sink to see if the water seeps through.

2 Trace the template from the back of the book and transfer it onto brown paper. Using tile cutters, cut the tiles into strips, squares and triangles (see page 4). Then lay the tesserae out on the pattern before you start glueing, as this is a complicated design.

3 Each space of this design requires a different cut of tesserae and so, there is a lot of nipping, scoring and snapping to do. You may find cutting tricky at first but it does become easier as you proceed. Using a water-soluble adhesive (see page 5), dab small amounts onto the paper with a paintbrush and stick the tesserae to the paper face down, grooved side up.

4 Mix up a quantity of adhesive (see page 5). Smear it neatly with the flat side of the scraper, on the base of the dish – if any sticks to the upright edge, clean it off. Smooth the surface evenly, then use the notched side to make grooves in it.

5 Carefully lower the entire circle onto the adhesive butting it up to the edges. Once the whole circle is down, gently wiggle the tiles into the adhesive to make sure they are grounded. Put aside for 24 hours to allow the adhesive to set.

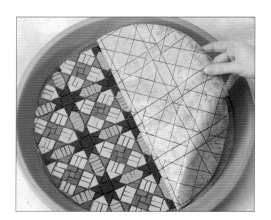

6 Wet the paper with a sponge and gently peel it away from the tiles (you may need to keep wetting the paper). Some tiles may stay on the paper – peel them off and stick them on separately.

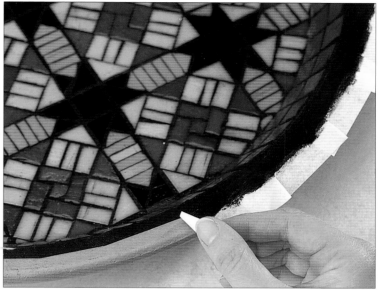

7 To mosaic the upright edge, butter whole red tiles with adhesive and push them into place. Make sure there is a gap surrounding each tile for the grout and that they are spaced as evenly as possible. When the circle is nearly complete, you may need to readjust the spacing between each tile (use only whole tiles). Prick out any excess adhesive from between the tesserae with a bradawl.

8 Stick pieces of masking tape along the top edge of the dish to make a neat circle. Mix water-resistant grout (see page 5) and apply it to the bottom of the dish and up the sides with a squeegee. Take the grout up to the masked edge and smooth it neatly. When the grout is almost dry, peel off the tape to reveal a neat edge. Leave the grout to set for 24 hours, then polish with a dry cloth.

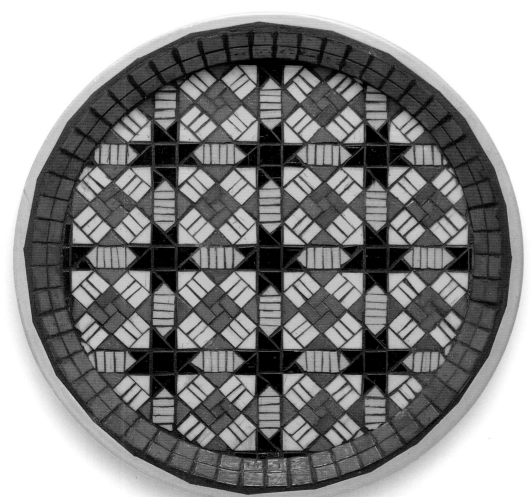

HINTS AND TIPS

▶ Because there are many different shapes in this design and you do not want to waste tiles through miscutting, follow the instructions on page 4 for *Cutting and Scoring*.

▶ It is advisable to cut all the tesserae before you start to lay them so that you do not have to break off mid-flow.

▶ Work in small sections when grouting your mosaic. This will enable you to wipe away any excess before it dries hard.

▶ If you are planning to fill this dish with water, do not place it directly on a treasured piece of furniture the first time in case any liquid seeps through.

INSPIRATIONAL IDEAS

The vivid colour combination chosen for this dish

is typically Moroccan. This intricate design would

work in any colourway: blues and greens would

be especially effective. Remember to use a grout

that matches your colours.

Basket Weave Paving Slabs

MATERIALS AND TOOLS

Tracing paper
Brown paper
Pencil
Ruler
Scissors
2 x 2cm (¾ x ¾in) glass tesserae:
one sheet of midnight blue and
electric blue, and quarter sheet of
brilliant white
Mosaic nippers
Surgical gloves and rubber gloves
Safety glasses
Mask
PVA waterproof exterior glue
Fine paintbrush
40 x 40cm (1⅓ x 1⅓ft)
paving slab/s
Concrete sealant and brush
Three buckets for mixing
Grey exterior powder adhesive
and additive
Trowel
3mm (¼in) notched trowel
Sponge
Bradawl or prodding tool
Grey exterior powder grout
and additive
Squeegee
Cloth

GLASS TESSERAE COLOURS

Brilliant white – *20.10(1) [EU]*
Electric Blue – *20.23(1) [EU]*
Midnight Blue – *20.46(2) [EU]*
(See page 32 for key to suppliers)

Morocco is a country rich with diverse land- and seascape. To the south and east are Mauritania and Algeria, which share the heat of the Western Sahara with Morocco; travel northwards and you would reach the Mediterranean, which gives Morocco its link to Europe, and especially Spain. These garden paving slabs combine the vibrant blues and whites of the Mediterranean with a typically Islamic geometric design. The pattern is extremely simple to execute but the finished object looks deceptively complicated. It was inspired not only by Morocco's ancient ceramic and tile craftsmanship but also its tradition of textiles, rug making and basket weaving. By uniformly laying the tesserae in the pattern below, the end design gives the effect of being woven.

USING THE TEMPLATE

Detach the template from the back of the book. Turn the tracing over and go over the outline on the reverse in pencil. Turn the tracing back over and position it on the brown paper.
Trace over the front, transferring the design to the brown paper.

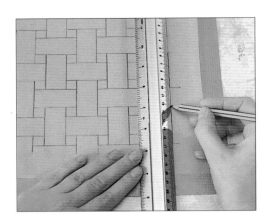

1 Trace the design onto brown paper using a ruler to make sure all the lines are straight. Cut away the excess brown paper to make the pattern the same size as the paving slab.

2 Wearing gloves, glasses and a mask for protection, cut the white glass tiles into halves. Place only a small portion of the tile in the nippers and pinch gently. Nip the halves into quarters; do not expect them to be exact, as this adds to the effect.

3 Water down some PVA glue (diluted in a ratio of about 60:40 glue to water). Apply a small blob of glue on the brown paper with a fine paintbrush and stick on the tiles correct side down, so that the grooved side is facing up. Be sure not to overload your brush with glue, because you only need very little. It is best to stick the blue whole tiles in place first and then drop in the white quarter tiles at the end. Prepare the sealant and powder adhesive (see page 5).

4 Take a concrete slab and brush on the concrete sealant. Trowel on the adhesive smoothing it right up to the edges, then use a notched trowel to create grooves. Make sure the adhesive is level – if not, re-groove the surface.

5 Line up the edge of the mosaic with one edge of the paving slab and very gently lower the sheet onto the slab. Keep checking the edges are straight. Once the whole sheet is down, smooth it out and push it down gently into the adhesive.

6 Leave to dry for 24 hours. With a wet sponge, gently wipe the paper all over so the whole sheet is wet. Gently peel the paper away. If some of the tesserae move or remain stuck to the paper, re-stick them to the adhesive individually.

7 Once the paper is removed, wipe the mosaic down with a damp sponge to remove any surface adhesive. Then, using a bradawl, or similar tool, prick out any excess adhesive that has squeezed up between the tesserae.

8 Mix a water-resistant grey grout (see page 5) – grey helps the colours of the mosaic stand out. Apply the grout with a squeegee, starting in the middle and working outwards. Take care to cover the edges of the slab as this helps to protect them and will preserve the life of your slab. Clean off the excess grout with a damp sponge. Buff with a soft cloth to reveal the lustre and shine of the glass tesserae.

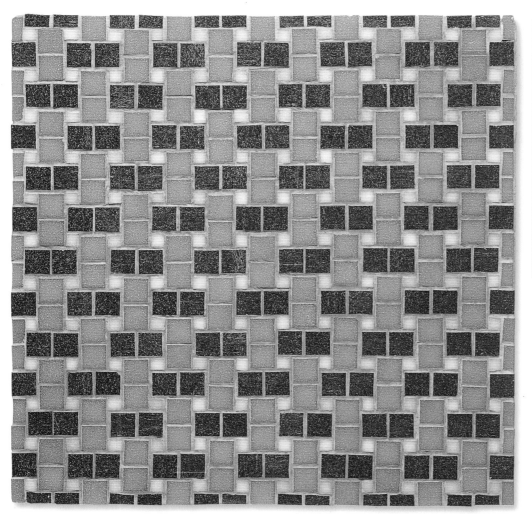

HINTS AND TIPS

▶ It is advisable to stick the tracing paper in place with adhesive tape to stop it moving about as you trace the design onto brown paper.

▶ Apply a concrete sealant to the slab/s before covering with adhesive. Ask advice from a local hardware shop as to which one to buy.

▶ Ensure that all your materials are suitable for outside use.

▶ If you want to create more than one mosaic paving slab, mix up enough grout to do all the slabs at once.

INSPIRATIONAL IDEAS

This paving stone would be good in any colour combination or mosaic materials. Be experimental and try a different palette for each stone slab. For example, terracotta and greens would create a warm, earthy look, or you could be bold using a bright contemporary palette. Try making several slabs in contrasting shades for a real splash of colour in your garden.

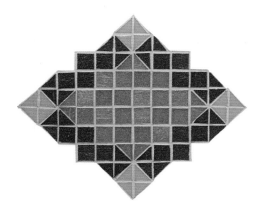

Geometric-patterned Tabletop

MATERIALS AND TOOLS

Tracing paper
Brown paper
Pencil
Ruler
2 x 2cm (³⁄₄ x ³⁄₄in) glass tesserae:
quarter sheet of lime, one and
half sheets of dark amethyst, three
sheets of lilac and one sheet of
rich amethyst (for the border)
Tile cutters
Surgical gloves and rubber gloves
Safety glasses
Mask
PVA glue
Fine paintbrush
Stanley knife
Plywood: 1cm (½in) depth x 60cm
(2ft) length x 60cm (2ft) width
Two buckets for mixing
Grey exterior powder adhesive
and additive
Trowel
3mm (¼in) notched trowel
Sponge
Bradawl or prodding tool
Grey exterior powder grout
and additive
Squeegee
Cloth
Metal table base

GLASS TESSERAE COLOURS

Lime citrus – A570 [RH]
Dark amethyst – 20.51(2) [RH]
Soft lilac – 20.25(2) [RH]
Rich amethyst – C290 [RH]
(See page 32 for key to suppliers)

The art of mosaic in Morocco has traditionally passed down from father to son for many centuries. Religion dictates that design throughout Morocco depicts no living thing, so geometric design dominates all forms of decoration. For this reason, Moroccan mosaic makers have always been talented mathematicians as well as incredible craftsmen. This tabletop pattern is a stunning example of skilled geometry. The scale used is designed to keep the cutting of tiles to a minimum, which makes this project extremely easy to make, and complementary shades of lilac and amethyst contrast effectively with a vibrant lime citrus. A plywood tabletop is used in conjunction with a simply constructed linear iron base, available from any metal artist; together they make the ideal setting for a Moroccan mint tea party.

USING THE TEMPLATE

Detach the template from the back of the book. Turn the tracing over and go over the outline on the reverse in pencil. Turn the tracing back over and position it on brown paper. Trace over the front, transferring the design onto the brown paper.

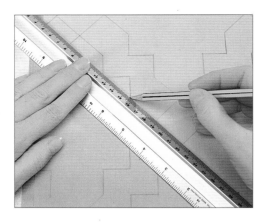

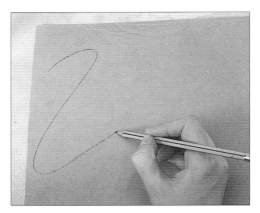

1 Trace the design from the template onto brown paper. Use a ruler to ensure straight lines. You might want to stick the template onto the paper to stop it moving about as you are tracing.

2 Turn over the brown paper. Take a pencil and draw an unbroken line from left to right across the paper. By doing this, when you come to stick the mosaic onto the board you will have clear registration marks to match up the four sections.

3 Cut the tesserae for the whole project: the lime citrus tiles need to be scored and snapped into triangles. The border is a combination of one row of whole tiles and one row of a half tiles, so nip the half tiles at this point too.

5 Once all the tiles are stuck in position, take a stanley knife and cut the paper into quarters. Flip the sections over so they are still in the right position and make sure all the pencil lines on the reverse correspond with the original layout.

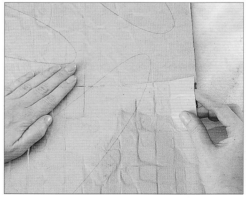

4 Water down some PVA glue and start to stick the tiles face down (grooved side up) onto the traced design – remember to stick the tiles to the matt side of the brown paper. Work in sections. If your triangles are not 100 per cent accurate they may need trimming carefully with the cutters – shave off any excess.

6 Evenly apply PVA glue to the plywood with a brush and wait for it to dry. Then, using the notched trowel, make grooves that the tesserae can bond to. Position each section on the board checking that the tiles do not hang over the edge.

7 Wet the back of the brown paper with a sponge and let the water soak in before peeling off the paper. Do not rush this process or the tiles will lift off with the paper; wait until it peels off easily. Some tiles may move slightly when the paper is removed – simply re-position these as you go. Prick out any excess adhesive from between the tesserae with a bradawl or similar tool.

8 Wearing protective gloves, make up some grout (see page 5). Spread it between the tiles using a squeegee pushing the grout into the gaps. Wipe off any excess grout and clean the surface with a damp sponge. A fine layer of residue will remain, but this will be cleaned off when you give the mosaic a final polish. With the aid of a friend lift and lower the mosaic onto the metal table base.

HINTS AND TIPS

▶ Be sure to wear a face mask when cutting tesserae to give protection against dust particles that can irritate your lungs.

▶ Dilute water-soluble PVA glue in a ratio of 60:40, glue to water.

▶ Use a trowel to apply adhesive to large areas such as this repetitive geometric design.

▶ When removing the design from the brown paper you may have to repeat the wetting process several times before the paper comes away easily.

▶ The wooden tabletop should be a few millimetres smaller than the metal frame to allow space for grout.

INSPIRATIONAL IDEAS

We used a specially designed base for our table, but you could just as easily use a reclaimed iron table. Simply drill a piece of plywood, cut to fit, to the existing tabletop and screw in place. For outside use, cover the plywood with a protective coating to protect it from the elements.

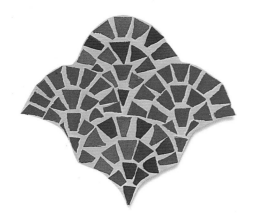

Shell-effect Skirting Border

This elaborate and ancient pattern, found throughout Morocco, creates a delicate, lattice effect along the length of a skirting board. It appears complicated but is incredibly easy to create. The key to success is to cut plenty of small triangles before you start working on the design. The basic shell pattern is built up from glossy burgundy and dark green porcelain tiles, which are set off with a beige grout. The shiny, reflective surface of the tiles is enhanced by the matt finish of the grout. When your skirting border is complete and in place, you will find that the surface shines and glistens, picking up and reflecting light. It shimmers and sparkles. Do not feel limited to using this design just along a skirting: it would work equally well decorating a picture frame or garden steps to evoke an exotic theme.

USING THE TEMPLATE

Detach the template from the back of the book. Turn the tracing paper over and go over the outline on the reverse in pencil. Turn it back over and place it over the MDF. Trace over the front, transferring your design onto the board. You will need to reuse this template to create enough sections to cover the length of skirting.

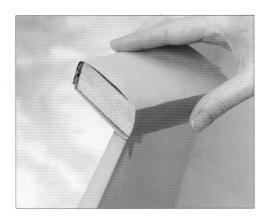

1 Take each section of wood and sand the edges. Apply two coats of PVA glue to the wood. Drill a hole in all four corners of each section of wood, then drill over the hole with a countersink piece. This will prevent the screws from protruding.

2 Trace the design from the template and transfer it onto each wood section using a pencil. Tracing onto a surface that has been covered with PVA can be difficult, so you may need to re-trace the marks freehand to make them easier to see.

3 Score lines along each tile using the cutter blade of the tile cutters, then use the snapper part to break them into strips. Remember to wear protective goggles in case of flying splinters and a mask to stop the inhalation of tile dust.

4 Secure each strip between the pincers of the mosaic nippers and nip at a 45-degree angle one way and 45-degrees the other. This creates little V-shaped pieces with flat bottoms ready to form the arches within the shell shape.

5 Draw a shell shape on a piece of paper and practise positioning the tesserae. This way you will know roughly how many pieces are required per arch. This is not a precise science and each section must be treated as a separate space.

6 Mix up a quantity of adhesive (see page 5) and trowel it neatly onto one shell shape. Position the tesserae, piece by piece, beginning at the top of the shell. This way you work in arches from top to bottom. It is important that there are the same number of rows and a single piece at the bottom of each shell shape.

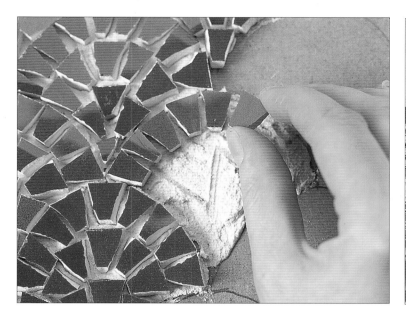 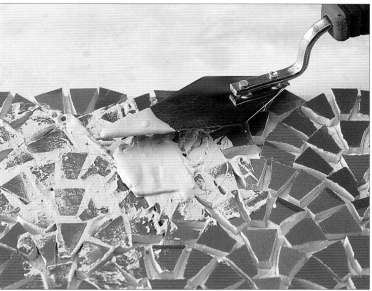

7 To complete the project, work in rows of shell shapes, colour by colour, from top to bottom. Take it slowly and calmly working methodically in one direction. Remember to leave drill holes uncovered. Leave to dry for 24 hours before pricking out the excess adhesive with a bradawl or similar prodding tool.

8 Mix some grout (see page 5) and trowel it into the gaps. Clean off the excess with a damp sponge. Wearing protective gloves, smooth the grout with your fingers over the top edge of the skirting so that the wood is covered and it is slightly domed: this adds to the rustic, Moroccan look. Leave the grout to dry for 24 hours. For fixing the mosaic to the wall see *Hints and Tips* (below).

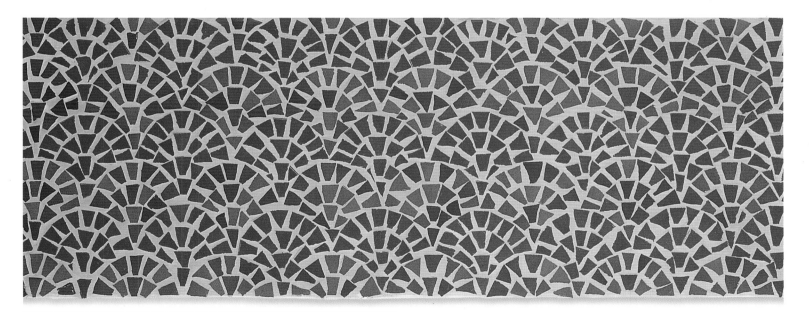

HINTS AND TIPS

▶ Tiles cutters are the best tool for cutting tiles of this size, as they score a guideline before making the cut. Scoring weakens the tile so that it breaks exactly where you want and not randomly at an angle.

▶ You will need to prepare many more tesserae than you might think for this project – the edges of most tiles are slightly bevelled making them unsuitable for this pattern, so there will be some wastage.

▶ Once your grout is dry, fix the mosaic to the wall. With an electric drill, drill holes in the wall in the same position as those in the mosaic and fit rawl plugs, then screw the mosaic in place. Mix up a small amount of adhesive and stick the tesserae over the area covering the screws. Leave to dry for 24 hours. Prick out excess adhesive with a bradawl, grout, wipe clean and polish.

INSPIRATIONAL IDEAS

This pattern lends itself to experimentation with different colour combinations. Creating each semi-circle in a different colourway would produce a vibrant and very modern mosaic. This design would work well for a floor mosaic – just reuse the template to create a repeating pattern.

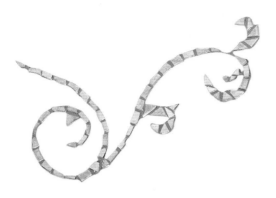

Gilded Minaret Mirror

MATERIALS AND TOOLS

Two pieces MDF: 1cm (½in)
depth x 60cm (2ft) length
x 28cm (11in) width
Pencil and ruler
Jigsaw
Tracing paper
Electric drill
PVA glue
Paintbrush
G-cramps or heavy weights
2 x 2cm (¾ x ¾in) tesserae: two
sheets of blue glass and
100 gold leaf tesserae
Mosaic nippers
Tile cutters
Surgical gloves and rubber gloves
Safety glasses
Mask
Two buckets for mixing
Grey powder adhesive
and additive
Trowel
Fine paintbrush
Abrasive paper
Bradawl or prodding tool
Grey powder grout and additive
Squeegee
Sponge
Cloth
47 x 19cm (1½ft x 7½in) mirror
47 x 19cm (1½ft x 7½in) hardboard
Panel pins and pin hammer

TESSERAE COLOURS

Midnight blue with gold fleck –
20.30(4) [EU]
English gold leaf – *[MS]*
(See page 32 for key to suppliers)

T his exquisite mirror combines a bold architectural outline with a delicate and intricate design. The result is an authentic-looking product of North Africa. The undulating design is reminiscent of Arabic script but with an organic essence, as it twists and twines its way around the frame. Although this is one of the more complicated projects in the book it is relatively easy once you get started, so do not be afraid to take on the challenge. Once you have mastered the scoring and snapping of the tiles it will be plain sailing. Whether resting on a mantlepiece in streaming sunshine or illuminated by candles at night, this mirror, with its midnight blue and gold leaf glass will conjure up the atmosphere, magic and mystery of Arabian Nights.

USING THE TEMPLATE

Detach the template from the back of the book. Turn the tracing paper over and go over the outline on the reverse in pencil. Turn the tracing back over and place it on the first piece of MDF: trace the border design over the front, transferring the design onto the MDF. Lift the tracing off and place it on the second piece of MDF and repeat tracing the minaret shape.

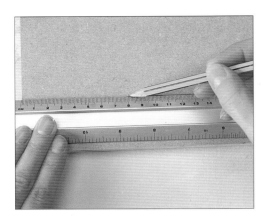

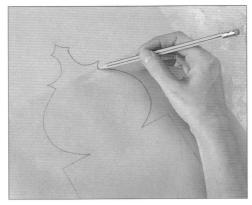

HINTS AND TIPS

▶ When tracing the curly pattern onto the mirror frame you may need to draw over the outline again because the PVA glue is a difficult surface to mark with pencil.

▶ If your adhesive outline dries before you get a chance to cover it with gold tesserae, simply rub it off with abrasive paper and start the outline again.

▶ Set yourself a small section to complete at a time – do not try to mosaic too much in one go, it will probably take a few sittings to finish.

▶ To attach the mirror into the frame, first paint the back of the frame black, paying special attention to the edges of the minaret. Slot in the mirror and hardboard backing. Then secure with panel pins, gently hammering them into the side of the frame so that the pins prevent the mirror and backing from falling out.

1 To make the mirror frame, take one piece of MDF and measure 4cm (1½in) in from the bottom and sides. Make several marks along these edges. Along the top, measure in 8cm (2in) and make marks. Join up all the marks to form a rectangle. Using a jigsaw, cut out this rectangle shape.

2 Using the template at the back of the book, trace the outline of the minaret onto the second piece of wood. Be sure to centre the design. Remember to use a soft pencil for the reverse tracing as it will maximize the carbon on the back and give a stronger traced line.

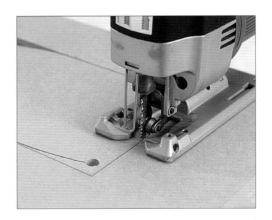

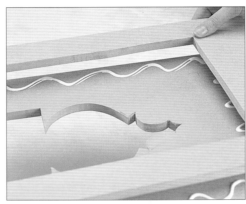

3 Drill a hole in the second piece of MDF, insert the jigsaw and cut away the minaret. Cut the straight lines first, then guide the jigsaw gently around the curves. You may have to drill extra holes to get into the tightest corners. Do not push the jigsaw to speed up this part – the MDF will cut easily if you let the jigsaw proceed at its own pace.

4 Squeeze a good quantity of strong PVA glue onto the back of the second piece of MDF (the minaret shape) keeping within the confines of the border. Cramp the two pieces of MDF together, or position a heavy object on top, and leave to dry. With a paintbrush, apply a layer of PVA as a sealant. Leave to dry until the glue is transparent.

5 Using mosaic nippers, cut the blue glass tiles into halves and then quarters. You will need these for the inside edge of the mirror. It doesn't matter if the shapes are irregular or if they shatter. This design can accommodate a variety of irregular shapes. Cut lots of small triangles at different angles. Keep all the bits that splinter off as they will always find a home somewhere.

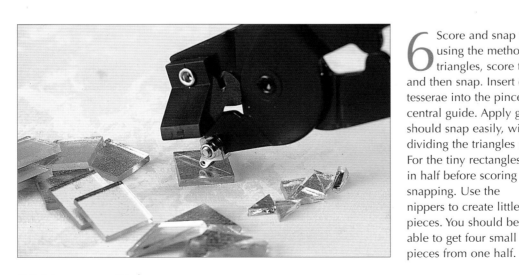

6 Score and snap the gold leaf tesserae with tile cutters using the method described on page 4. To make tiny triangles, score the tesserae from corner to corner and then snap. Insert only around a quarter of the tesserae into the pincers, using the scored line as a central guide. Apply gentle pressure and the tesserae should snap easily, with minimal shattering. Keep dividing the triangles until they are small enough. For the tiny rectangles, divide the tiles in half before scoring and snapping. Use the nippers to create little pieces. You should be able to get four small pieces from one half.

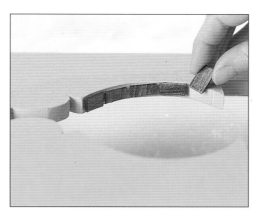

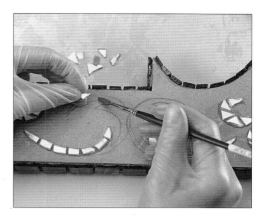

7 Mix up a small quantity of adhesive (see page 5). Starting on the outside edge, butter whole tiles and hold each one in position for a couple of seconds. Work your way around the whole frame. If, when you are nearing an edge, it becomes clear that a gap is too small for a whole tile, add a half tile somewhere along the line.

8 Using either halves or quarters, move on to the inside edge of the minaret. The straight edges are easy and the curves are slightly trickier. Butter each mosaic piece as before with adhesive and hold in place. Leave to dry for at least three hours before starting the main design.

9 Trace the curly pattern onto the mirror frame. Make up a quantity of runny adhesive and use a fine paintbrush to apply it to the tracing. Do this in lines and work quite quickly before it dries. If you are a bit optimistic and the adhesive dries before you get there, sand it off and start again.

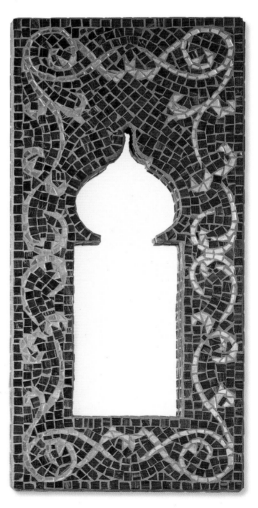

10 Fill in the background with quarter blue tiles, working in lines against the gold curves to give them the illusion of movement. You will need a lot of irregular pieces and triangles to fill in all the gaps. Leave to dry for 24 hours before pricking out the excess adhesive with a bradawl or similar tool. Mix up a quantity of grout (see page 5), spread it over the design with a squeegee, pushing it into the gaps. Wipe excess away with a damp sponge. Leave to dry for 24 hours and polish with a cloth. See *Hints and Tips* for attaching the mirror.

INSPIRATIONAL IDEAS

For a glamourous interior, the curly gold design could be used as a skirting border and continued around the door frame.

ACKNOWLEDGEMENTS

My thanks to Mum, Roy, Siana, Jonnie and
Rafe Yewdall, Christophe Bourillon for all his help
with my computer, Natasha, Sam and Bertie Stocks,
Serisa and Phoebe Janes for hand modelling,
Guy and Beth Butterwick, Alexander Bullock,
Melanie Shirley, Sarah and Peter Jenkins, Caroline,
Graeme and the Feelgood Studios, and Pasha.

Text on pages 2–7 written by Donna Reeves.

SUPPLIERS

Edgar Udny & Co Ltd [EU]
314 Balham High Road
London SW17 7AA
Tel: 020 8767 8181
Fax: 020 8767 7709

*Suppliers of vitreous glass, smalti, gold and
silver leaf, and ceramics as well as fixing
materials and gummed brown paper. Mail
order service available.*

Reed Harris [RH]
Riverside House
27 Carnwath Road
London SW6 3HR
Tel: 020 7736 751
Fax: 020 7736 2988

*Supplier of household tiles, porcelain and marble
tesserae as well as sealants, tools, adhesives and
grout. Mail order service available.*

Mosaic Workshop [MS]
443–449 Holloway Road
London N7 6LJ
Tel: 020 7263 2997

On the Tiles
2 Parkville Road
London SW6 7BX
Tel: 020 7385 5480

Suppliers of H&R Johnson tesserae [HRJ]

Published by Murdoch Books®
First published in 2000

ISBN 1 85391 814 8
A catalogue record of this book is
available from the British Library.
© Text, design, photography and illustrations
Murdoch Books (UK) Ltd 2000.

Commissioning Editor: Natasha Martyn-Johns
Project Editor: Sarah Wilde
Designer: Cathy Layzell
Photographer: Graeme Ainscough
Stylist: Caroline Davies

CEO: Robert Oerton
Publisher: Catie Ziller
Publishing Manager: Fia Fornari
Production Manager: Lucy Byrne

Group General Manager: Mark Smith
Group CEO/Publisher: Anne Wilson

Colour separation by Colourscan, Singapore
Printed in Singapore by Imago

Murdoch Books (UK) Ltd
Ferry House, 51–57 Lacy Road,
Putney, London, SW15 1PR
Tel: +44 (0)20 8355 1480, Fax: +44 (0)20 8355 1499
Murdoch Books (UK) Ltd is a subsidiary of
Murdoch Magazines Pty Ltd.

Murdoch Books®
GPO Box 1203
Sydney NSW 1045
Tel: +61 (0)2 9692 2347, Fax: +61 (0)2 9692 2559
Murdoch Books® is a trademark of
Murdoch Magazines Pty Ltd.